SHALLOW GRAVE

SHALLOW GRAVE

John Hodge

faber and faber

First published in 1996
by Faber & Faber Ltd
Bloomsbury House,
74–77 Great Russell Street,
London, WC1B 3DA
This edition first published in 2000

Photoset by Parker Typesetting Services, Leicester

Printed and bound by CPI Group (UK) Ltd, Croydon, CR0 4YY

A CIP record for this book
is available from the British Library

ISBN 978–0–571–20294–2

6 8 10 9 7 5

CONTENTS

INTRODUCTION

I began writing *Shallow Grave* in the spring of 1991. If I had known then what I know now about the coalition of fortune and favour that must occur before a script becomes a film, I would not have bothered. I knew nothing and no one. I naïvely assumed that all I had to do was write what I liked and all the necessary people would fall into place. They would take the script from my hands and turn it into the film I wanted to see. That this is more or less exactly what happened is a tribute to the beneficial effects of ignorance.

I had this idea about three people in a flat and a stranger and a bag of money and that seemed to me like a film, so I began writing. With a view to an end-of-career auction, the first draft of *Shallow Grave* was hand-written on table napkins, backs of envelopes, etc. I showed it to my sister who introduced me to a guy called Andrew Macdonald who said that he was a 'producer'. This was a lie. He told me that he had worked in Hollywood as a script editor. This was a lie. He told me that he had met Bridget Fonda; that he knew Bridget Fonda well, and implied, more or less, that he had enjoyed a tabloid celebrity-style on-off relationship with Bridget Fonda for several years and that it was only a matter of time before I saw her on the cover of *Hello!* magazine under the headline 'Coping without Andrew: Bridget Fonda's Inner Strength'. He assured me that she would star in our film, along with Ray Liotta and Bill Murray (the two male leads I had in mind). Need I say that this was all one big lie?

I soon discovered the true nature of Macdonald's work 'in television' when I visited the set of *Taggart* and was witness to the spectacle of Bridget Fonda's on-off lover replenishing the store of Andrex in the extras' toilets and then spooning tuna to the leading lady's cat.

But Macdonald and I established a healthy working relationship. I would write a new draft of the script which he would then read and then return with a tactful critique like, 'The second half isn't up to much.' Holding back the tears, I would review the section in question and, to my regular irritation, find myself in agreement. I then indulged in orgies of bloodletting, striking out subplots, characters, and locations, and a couple of months later we would do it all over again.

After about a year and half of this we found ourselves in the offices of Channel Four facing two responsible adults who liked the script but wanted to know just who did we think we were. I would have immediately confessed to our status as bona fide no-hopers but Macdonald intervened and revealed why he is a producer and I am not. I sat in awed silence while he calmly described his background in 'film' and 'television': the formative experiences at Pinewood and Shepperton (back in the days when there was British film industry, of course), the Hollywood years, the loss of faith in the studio system, the return to small-scale, low-budget short film-making, the directorial dabbling, and the limitless commercial and artistic vision. The only thing he missed out was the on-off love affair with Bridget Fonda. It was a marvellous performance. We were instructed to return with a new draft, a budget, and a director.

So while I sweated out another new draft, Macdonald spent the next two months having lunch, which is apparently the accepted method of finding a director.

Danny Boyle was not what I expected. Where were the jodhpurs, the beret, and the megaphone? In conversation he came across as a man of sensitivity and endless patience but with a thuggish streak and a certain low, animal cunning: in short, a man who could work with actors. Any doubts I might have harboured were blown away on our first return to the responsible adults, when Boyle answered the question of how he would direct the film by saying that it would be 'witty, but not expressionist'. I have often pondered on the meaning of this phrase, wondering whether or not it would be altered by rearranging the words.

A few more rewrites were undertaken as the summer drifted by and filming drew ever nearer. My involvement gradually faded out until I reached the role of constitutional monarch, consulted on everything on the understanding that the answer would be 'yes'. This is the writer's lot: anyone who doesn't like it should learn either to lie or to work with actors. I began to plan my retirement.

John Hodge, November 1995

Shallow Grave

INT. DAY

A blurred image forms on a white screen. A horizontal strip of face, eyes motionless and unblinking.

DAVID
(*voice-over*)
Take trust, for instance, or friendship: these are the important things in life, these are the things that matter, that help you on your way. If you can't trust your friends, well, what then?

EXT. DAWN

A series of fast-cut static scenes of empty streets.

DAVID
(*voice-over*)
This could have been any city: they're all the same.

A rapid, swerving track along deserted streets and down narrow lanes and passageways. Accompanied by soundtrack and credits.

The track ends outside a solid, fashionable Edinburgh tenement.

INT. STAIRWELL. DAY

At the door of a flat on the third floor of the tenement. The door is dark, heavy wood and on it is a plastic card embossed with names of the three tenants. They are Alex Law, David Stevens and Juliet Miller.

A man climbs the stair and reaches the door. He is Cameron Clark, thin and in his late twenties with a blue anorak and lank, greasy hair. He is carrying an awkwardly bulky plastic bag. Cameron gives the doorbell an ineffectual ring and then stands back, shifting nervously from foot to foot until the door is answered.

CAMERON
Hello, I've come about the room.

Cameron enters and the door closes.

INT. LIVING ROOM. DAY

*David, Alex and Juliet sit in a line on the sofa directly opposite
Cameron, who shifts uneasily in his armchair. Alex checks some items
on a clipboard before speaking.*

ALEX

What's his name?

DAVID

I don't know – Campbell or something?

JULIET

Cameron.

ALEX

Cameron?

JULIET

Yes.

ALEX
(to Juliet)

Really?

4

CAMERON

That's right.

ALEX
(*to Cameron*)

What?

Cameron is not sure what to say.

Well, Cameron, are you comfortable?

CAMERON

Oh, yes, thanks.

ALEX

Good. Well, you've seen the flat?

CAMERON

Yes.

ALEX

And you like it?

CAMERON

Oh, yes, it's great.

ALEX

Yes. It is, isn't it? We all like it. And the room's nice too, don't you think?

CAMERON

Yes.

ALEX

Spacious, quiet, bright, well appointed, all that sort of stuff, all that crap.

CAMERON

Well, yes.

ALEX

So tell me, Cameron, what on earth – just tell me, because I want to know – what on earth could make you think that we would want to share this flat with someone like you?

INT. STAIRWELL. DAY

As Cameron plods slowly down the stairs, his shoes striking out against the stone steps, Alex's criticisms continue.

                    ALEX
                 (*voice-over*)
I mean, my first impression, and they're rarely wrong, is that you have none of the qualities that we normally seek in a prospective flatmate. I'm talking here about things like presence, charisma, style and charm, and I don't think we're being unreasonable. Take David here, for instance: a chartered accountant he may be, but at least he tries hard. The point is, I don't think you're even trying.

Cameron has reached the bottom of the stairs. He opens the main door.

And, Cameron – I mean this – good luck!

Cameron leaves and the main door closes behind him.

Do you think he was upset?

*[INT. STAIRWELL. DAY

Outside the door of the flat a prim, matronly Woman in her early twenties rings the bell.

INT. HALL. DAY

Inside the hall of the flat, David approaches the door to open it. Freeze-frame.

                    ALEX
                 (*voice-over*)
David likes to keep spare shoelaces in sorted pairs in a box marked, not just 'shoelaces', but 'spare shoelaces'.

David opens the door to the Woman.

                    WOMAN
I've come to see about the room.

*Cut from completed film.

6

INT. STAIRWELL. DAY

Outside the door of the flat a young Goth girl, aged about twenty, rings the doorbell.

INT. HALL. DAY

Inside the hall of the flat Alex approaches the door to open it. Freeze-frame.

JULIET
(*voice-over*)
Alex is a vegetarian. Do you know why? Because he feels it provides an interesting counterpoint to his otherwise callous personality. It doesn't. He thinks he's the man for me. He isn't, though there was a time when, well, there was a time when . . .

Alex opens the door to the Goth.

GOTH
I've come about this room.

INT. STAIRWELL. DAY

At the door of the flat a Man aged about thirty-five rings the bell.

INT. HALL. DAY

Inside the hall of the flat Juliet approaches the door to open it. Freeze-frame.

DAVID
(*voice-over*)
Like one of those stupid posters – you know, a gorilla cuddling a hedgehog, caption 'love hurts' – that's what I think of when I think of Juliet.

Juliet opens the door to the Man.

MAN
I've come about the room.]

INT. LIVING ROOM. DAY

In the living room each of the 'candidates' is interviewed individually with the same seating arrangements as before (i.e. the trio on the sofa and the applicant on the chair). What we see are briskly intercut excerpts from each of these interviews. We do not get the responses to the questions, although we may see some facial reaction.

All of David's questions are to the Woman.

All of Alex's questions are to the Goth.

All of Juliet's questions are to the Man.

DAVID

All right, just a few questions.

ALEX

I'd like to ask you about your hobbies.

JULIET

Why do you want a room here?

DAVID

Do you smoke?

ALEX

When you slaughter a goat and wrench its heart out with your bare hands, do you then summon hellfire?

JULIET

I mean, what are you actually doing here? What is the hidden agenda?

DAVID

Do a little freebase maybe, from time to time?

ALEX

Or maybe just phone out for a pizza?

JULIET

Look, it's a fairly straightforward question. You're either divorced or you're not.

DAVID

OK, I'm going to play you just a few seconds of this tape – I'd like

you to name the song, the lead singer and three hit singles
subsequently recorded by him with another band.

ALEX
When you get up in the morning, how do you decide which shade
of black to wear?

JULIET
Now, let me get this straight. This affair that you're not having, is
it not with a man or not with a woman?

DAVID
Turning very briefly to the subject of corporate finance – no, this
is important. Leveraged buy-outs – a good thing or a bad thing?

*[
ALEX
With which of the following figures do you most closely identify:
Joan of Arc, Eva Braun or Marilyn Monroe?

JULIET
It's just that you strike me as a man trapped in a crisis of
emotional direction, afflicted by a realization that the partner of
your dreams is, quite simply, just that.]

DAVID
Did you ever kill a man?

ALEX
And when did anyone last say to you these exact words: 'You are
the sunshine of my life'?

*[
JULIET
OK, so A has left you, B is ambivalent, you're still seeing C but D
is the one you yearn for. What are we to make of this? If I were
you, I'd ditch the lot. There's a lot more letters in the alphabet of
love.]

DAVID
And what if I told you that I was the Antichrist?

*Cut from completed film.

9

INT. SQUASH COURT. EVENING

In a sports centre Juliet sits outside a glass-walled squash court. She is ready to play, but at present is watching Alex and David, who are inside the court.

INT. SQUASH COURT. EVENING

Inside the squash court, Alex is about to serve.

                    ALEX
Squash is often used as a metaphor to represent a struggle for personal domination.

                    DAVID
Serve.

                    ALEX
I was trying to educate you.

                    DAVID
Just serve.
*[ALEX
In the same fashion as chess.

                    DAVID
What?

                    ALEX
Chess. Chess is often used as well.

                    DAVID
Will you shut up and play.

                    ALEX
You're a bad loser.

                    DAVID
I haven't lost yet.]

   Alex serves.

*Cut from completed film.

10

INT. SQUASH COURT. EVENING

The squash-court door opens and David walks out past Juliet as Alex stands behind, jabbing his finger at him.

ALEX

Defeat, defeat, defeat – sporting, personal, financial, professional, sexual, everything. Next.

Juliet walks in and closes the door.

INT. SQUASH COURT. EVENING

Inside the squash court Alex is about to serve.

ALEX

Did you know –

JULIET

Just serve, Alex.

Alex serves.

INT. JULIET'S CAR (A MINI). NIGHT

Alex sits in the back, drinking.

Juliet is driving. David sits beside her.

ALEX

I wasn't trying to win.

There is no response from Juliet.

I don't wish to devalue your victory, but I just want you to know: I wasn't trying to win.

DAVID

Victory is the same as defeat. It's giving in to destructive competitive urges.

ALEX

You learn that in your psychotherapy group?

DAVID

Discussion group, Alex, discussion.

JULIET

I thought you stopped going.

ALEX

Yeah, he had too many of those urges. You of all people should know that.

Alex leans close to Juliet. Juliet brakes abruptly and, as Alex flies forwards, elbows him in the chest.

God, you two are just so sensitive. All I'm doing is implying some sort of sordid, ugly, sexual liaison. Why, I'd be proud of that sort of thing.

JULIET

Maybe you should go, Alex. You'll meet someone wonderful.

ALEX

For my life? At a discussion group? I think not.

JULIET

For the flat.

ALEX

No. Be someone else like him. One is enough. And what happened to that girl, that friend of yours, the one that came round. I liked her. I really felt we had something. She could have moved in. We had chemistry.

JULIET

She hated you –

ALEX

Well, she had problems –

JULIET

– more than anyone she has ever met. In her whole life.

ALEX

– I'd be the first to point that out. In all kindness I would. But, like they say, you know, she's got to want to change, hasn't she?

INT. STAIRWELL. DAY

Outside the door of the flat Hugo rings the bell and waits. Juliet opens the door. Hugo is in his early thirties, tall, dark and bohemian in appearance.

JULIET

You must be Hugo.

HUGO

You must be Juliet.

JULIET

Would you like to come in?

HUGO

I'd be delighted.

Hugo walks in and Juliet closes the door quite deliberately behind him.

INT. VACANT ROOM. DAY

Hugo looks around, pleased at what he sees, while Juliet watches him. He sits on the edge of the bed.

HUGO

It's nice.

JULIET

Would you like to see the rest?

INT. LIVING ROOM. DAY

Hugo is seated on the sofa, Juliet sits opposite on an armchair.

JULIET

What do you do?

HUGO

Well, I've been away for a bit, travelling, that sort of thing, and now I'm trying to write a novel.

JULIET

What's it about?

HUGO

A priest who dies.

JULIET

I see.

HUGO

Yeah. Well, maybe I'll change it.

JULIET

No.

HUGO

Yes, I mean, who wants to read about another dead priest? It's about some other guy, some guy who's not a priest, who doesn't die. You see, it's better already.

JULIET

Writing seems easy.

HUGO

It's a breeze.

> *The telephone begins to ring out in the hall. Juliet does not move and at first says nothing. Hugo looks at her and towards the door leading to the hall. After several rings, Juliet speaks.*

JULIET

Do you think you could answer that?

HUGO

The telephone?

It continues to ring.

JULIET

Yes, the telephone, but if it's for me, I'm not in.

HUGO

You're not in.

JULIET

No.

HUGO

All right.

Hugo stands up. The ringing continues.

INT. HALL. DAY

Hugo lifts the phone. He turns to face Juliet and looks her in the eye as he lies on her behalf.

HUGO

Hello. Yes. Who's calling please? Well, I'm sorry, but she's not in right now. I don't know. Would you like to leave a message?

Hugo replaces the receiver.

It was some guy called Brian.

JULIET

Did he sound upset?

HUGO

A little bit. Is that good or bad?

JULIET

It's an improvement.

The telephone begins to ring again.

HUGO

Shall I answer it?

No, just leave it. He knows I must be at home. I'm working nights this week.

The telephone continues to ring.

HUGO

Working nights?

JULIET

I'm a doctor.

HUGO

And he's a patient of yours?

JULIET

No, but he needs treatment.

HUGO

For what?

JULIET

For a certain weakness.

HUGO

The human condition.

JULIET

You know about it?

HUGO

I write about it.

JULIET

And that's not the same thing?

HUGO

No, but like all novelists, I'm in search of the self.

INT. KITCHEN. MORNING

Juliet, dressed and fatigued, sits at the table sipping a cup of coffee. Alex is also seated at the table, but wearing an old dressing-gown and munching at cornflakes while he reads a newspaper and talks at the same time. An array of other papers is spread over the table.

ALEX

Has he tried down behind the fridge. I mean, that's where I normally find things.

JULIET

He seemed like a nice guy, Alex.

Juliet gets up and leaves the kitchen. The sound of a bath running is heard.

ALEX

I'm not saying he didn't seem like a nice guy. All I'm saying is, it's a bit strange, and this search for the self, and what's he on about, you know.

Alex hears the mail falling through the door and stands up to leave the kitchen and get it.

JULIET
(*calling from outside*)

He didn't seem strange, Alex. He seemed, you know –

INT. BATHROOM. MORNING

Juliet watches the bath fill.

JULIET

. . . interesting.

INT. KITCHEN, MORNING

Alex considers her reply.

ALEX

Interesting. Interesting.

INT. HALL. MORNING

Alex is walking through the hall to the door, muttering 'interesting' to himself. As he passes the phone it starts to ring. He stops and lifts it.

ALEX

Hello. No, she's not in. No. No. No. No idea.

Alex replaces the receiver and walks on to the door.

JULIET
(*from the bathroom*)

Who was it?

ALEX

I don't know. He sounded Swedish. Do you know any Swedish men? Maybe it was just the emotion.

Alex picks up the mail and looks through it. As he does so, David emerges from his room, dressed for work.

What do you think?

DAVID

About what?

ALEX

About this guy, this Hugo person.

DAVID

I don't have time.

ALEX

I'm only asking what you think.

DAVID

I don't have the time to discuss it now. I don't care so long as he's not a freak.

David opens the door. Alex hands him an envelope.

ALEX

This is for you. It's your mother's handwriting, so I didn't open it. I don't like reading about your father's constipation.

David snatches the letter and leaves, closing the door.

Alex walks back across the hall, opening one of the letters and reading it quickly.

JULIET
(*calling from the bathroom*)

So we'll meet him, then?

ALEX

What? Oh, yeah, sure, if you want. I tell you, every letter this guy writes to you is the same: they all begin like pure love and descend into open pornography. 'I dream of your thighs, the soft touch of your white skin leading me in desire, while I, aroused and inflamed –'

Juliet's head and arm appear around the bathroom door. She attempts to grab the letter. Alex plays at holding it just beyond her reach, before letting her take it.

ALEX

Aroused and inflamed.

JULIET

Alex.

ALEX

He even signs them, in his own name, can you believe it? I'd sign someone else's name. I'd sign his name. If I wrote them, that is. Which I don't.

INT. LIVING ROOM. EVENING

Alex, David, Juliet and Hugo sit round a table towards the end of a meal. Alcohol has been consumed. Bowls containing the last of the food sit on the table, being picked at occasionally. Alex dispenses wine mainly into his own glass, alternating with Macallan malt whisky, of which he pours generous measures.

ALEX

Interesting.

HUGO

I see.

ALEX

Yeah, well, that was what she said. Interesting. That's why you're here, you see.

DAVID

Normally I don't meet people, unless I already know them.

HUGO

I see.

                    DAVID

People can be so cruel.

                    ALEX

So, uh . . .

                    HUGO

What?

                    ALEX

What?

                    HUGO

You were going to say something.

                    ALEX

What was I trying to say? Oh, yes, I think, we think, or at least I
suppose we think – am I right?

                    JULIET

Just get on with it, Alex.

*[DAVID
Keep it going, Alex. You're unstoppable now.]

*Cut from completed film.

                    20

ALEX

We think it's fine.

Alex starts eating again. The others watch him expectantly. David coughs.

It's OK. There's no problem.

HUGO

You mean I can have the room?

*[ALEX
Well, that's what I said, isn't it?

DAVID

He made it clear.

ALEX

Why, thank you, David.]

JULIET

Yes, you can have the room.

Alex pours yet more alcohol.

ALEX

I'm not usually drunk.

JULIET

Not usually this drunk.

DAVID

Only on expenses.

ALEX

It's true. A newspaper is paying for all this. All this. A newspaper . . .

With exaggerated scorn, Alex knocks over a glass of wine.

JULIET

In a moment he's going to tell you he could have been someone –

ALEX

It was you, Juliet, it was you –

*Cut from completed film.

                    JULIET

– instead of what he is –

                    ALEX

What I am.

                    JULIET

– which is –

                    ALEX

– which is a hack.

                    JULIET

The man we know and love.

                    ALEX

A miserable, burnt-out, empty shell of a –

    Alex pauses, looks at his drink, then at Juliet.

Know and love?

                    JULIET

Yeah.

                    ALEX

I think you're lying.

                    JULIET

You're right.

                    ALEX

You see, they don't really know me.

                    JULIET

No, Alex, we don't really love you.

    Alex smiles at Juliet and drinks again.

                    ALEX

Can you afford this place?

                    HUGO

Yeah.

    Hugo reaches into his pocket and pulls out a thick bundle of notes, which he places in front of Alex. Alex leans over and sniffs the notes.

DAVID

Can I ask you a question?

HUGO

Certainly.

DAVID

Have you ever killed a man?

HUGO

No.

DAVID

Well, that's fair enough, then.

Alex raises his head.

ALEX

Certainly smells like the real thing.

EXT. A STREET. NIGHT

At a cash dispenser a man in his thirties is taking out some money.

A younger man, Andy, stands beside him, looking around in a mildly agitated fashion.

As the money emerges, Andy assaults and robs the man. He starts by smashing his victim's face repeatedly against the cash dispenser until the Perspex is smeared with blood. When he has finished and the man lies on the ground, Andy takes the money and the card from the slots, then gets into a car which has pulled up alongside, driven by Tim.

INT. STAIRWELL. DAY

Hugo climbs the stairs, carrying two suitcases. He stops at the door of the flat and looks at a bunch of keys before selecting one, which he inserts in the door.

INT. HALL. DAY

Inside the flat. The door opens and Hugo lifts his cases in, kicking the door closed behind him.

INT. JULIET'S ROOM. DAY

Juliet sleeps, undisturbed by the closing of the door.

INT. HALL. DAY

Hugo walks across the hall and disappears into his room.

*[INT. HUGO'S ROOM. DAY

Hugo unpacks his bags. Included in his things are a few syringes and needles. All these he puts into the drawer beside his bed. He checks inside a second bag.

INT. HALL. DAY

Hugo dials a number on the telephone and awaits a reply.]

INT. JULIET'S ROOM. EVENING

Juliet is woken by her alarm clock. The time is five p.m.

INT. LIVING ROOM. NIGHT

Alex sits watching television, constantly changing channels. Juliet walks in, wearing a dressing gown. She watches Alex for a few moments.

                    JULIET
Have you seen Hugo?

                    ALEX
No. Any idea which channel he's on?

INT. HALL. MORNING

The telephone is ringing. Alex lifts the receiver. Again he is wearing his dressing gown and is on his way to pick up the mail.

                    ALEX
No, she's not in.

   Without waiting for any more, he replaces the receiver and walks to the door, where he picks up the mail. On his way back from the door,

*Cut from completed film.

David emerges, ready to go to work.

Have you seen him?

> DAVID

Alex, I don't have the time –

> ALEX

Yes or no, yes or no, yes or –

> DAVID

No.

David leaves, slamming the door.

INT. KITCHEN. MORNING

Alex returns to the kitchen, pausing only to knock at Hugo's door, which elicits no response. In the kitchen Juliet sits dressed for work, having just returned. He casually opens an envelope and glances at both sides of the letter before handing it to her.

> ALEX

David hasn't seen him either.

> JULIET

So I gathered.

> ALEX

Maybe he didn't like us.

> JULIET

David?

> ALEX

Hugo.

> JULIET

His car's still there.

> ALEX

He's got a car?

> JULIET

So what's wrong with that?

ALEX

What sort of car?

JULIET

Alex, how would I know? I'm just a girl.

ALEX

I will ask you once more, what sort of car –

JULIET

A blue one, OK. And it's still there.

INT. HALL. NIGHT

We see the door to Hugo's room, then Alex rapping sharply against it. David and Juliet stand behind him.

ALEX

Hugo. Hugo. Sorry about this, but can you open the door? It's us, Hugo, your flatmates and companions. Your new-found friends. He's not in. He's left and we'll probably never see him again.

JULIET

Alex, the key is in the keyhole on the other side.

ALEX

So?

JULIET

Open it.

ALEX

You want me to kick it open?

JULIET

Yes.

ALEX

Now?

JULIET

Yes.

ALEX

All right. No problem.

After a few rather ineffective kicks at the door, Alex turns to David.

You want a go?

INT. HUGO'S ROOM, NIGHT

Inside Hugo's room we see the door as David, outside, throws himself against it. At the third attempt the lock gives way and the door bursts open.

In the foreground at one side is the bed with a naked foot lying still and exposed.

When the door is open, David is first in, followed by the other two. There is a period of silent shock as they all contemplate Hugo's naked corpse. Alex opens a window.

DAVID

Is this what they always look like?

JULIET

Yes.

Juliet drapes a sheet over the body, covering it incompletely.

ALEX

I wonder how he did it?

JULIET

What?

ALEX

I wonder how he killed himself. I presume that that's what happened. What do you think?

Quite casually, Alex begins to open drawers and cupboards, emptying the contents on to the floor.

JULIET

Alex.

ALEX

What? What's wrong?

JULIET

What are you doing?

27

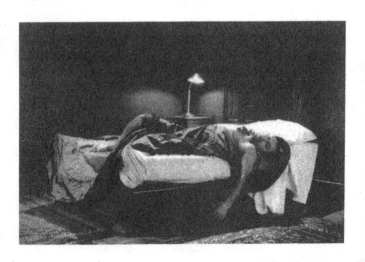

ALEX

I'm just looking.

JULIET

Don't.

ALEX

Don't look?

JULIET

No.

ALEX

Why not? What's wrong, Juliet? Aren't you curious? Don't you
wonder what he died from?

JULIET

No. The guy's dead. What more do you need?

ALEX

It's not every day I find a story in my own flat.

JULIET

That's not a story, it's a corpse.

*[
ALEX

Old newspaper proverb says dead human being is living story. Be
rational, please, and failing that be quiet.]

*In a drawer in a bedside cabinet, Alex finds needles, syringes and a
small bag of white powder. Without comment, he holds it up and
throws it on to the bed.*

*He reaches under the bed and pulls out a case, which he opens. It is
empty and he pushes it back under.*

DAVID

I've never seen a dead body before.

JULIET

Alex, I think it's about time for you to stop.

Alex continues to search. Juliet walks out.

*Cut from completed film.

INT. HALL. NIGHT

Juliet stands alone.

INT. HUGO'S ROOM. NIGHT

Alex continues his brisk search through Hugo's possessions while David looks on, appalled but speechless.

INT. HALL. NIGHT

Juliet listens to the sounds from the bedroom, then picks up the telephone. She dials 999 and waits for a reply. It rings and rings.

INT. HUGO'S ROOM, NIGHT.

Alex has found and opened a large Gladstone bag. Neither David nor we can see into it.

DAVID
I saw my grandmother, of course, but I don't suppose that counts, I mean, she was alive at the time.

ALEX
Can I show you something?

INT. HALL. NIGHT

Juliet awaits an answer.

Alex approaches Juliet with the open bag. She turns around and looks into it, then, seeing the contents, she replaces the receiver. As she does so, the Operator's voice is audible for a second.

OPERATOR
Hello, emergency services.

The telephone hits the cradle.

INT. KITCHEN. NIGHT

David, Alex and Juliet are seated in silence around the table. The bag, stacked with money, lies open on the table.

                              DAVID
No.

                              ALEX
Think about it.

                              DAVID
No.

                              ALEX
Come on, David.

                              DAVID
No.

                              ALEX
Juliet?

                              JULIET
No, Alex. It's, it's –

                              ALEX
What?

                              JULIET
Unfeasible.

                              ALEX
Is that all?

                              DAVID
You mean immoral.

                              ALEX
I'm only asking you both to think about it.

                              DAVID
It's a sick idea, Alex. It's sick.

                              ALEX
But don't tell me that you're not tempted by it. Don't tell me that
you're not interested. I know you well enough.

                              DAVID
You think so?

(*amused*)

All right, then, go ahead, telephone. Telephone the police. Try again. No one's going to stand in your way. Go ahead. Tell them there's a suitcase of money and you don't want it.

They sit in silence.

INT. HALL. MORNING

The flat is silent. Footsteps are heard outside the door and mail falls through the letter box.

INT. LIVING ROOM. DAY

The living room, empty.

INT. KITCHEN. DAY

The kitchen, empty. The bag of money still sits on the table.

INT. HUGO'S BEDROOM. DAY

His corpse still lies on the bed, covered as before, incompletely, by a sheet, with parts of his body still showing (a foot, a hand, part of his face or abdomen).

INT. NEWSPAPER OFFICE. DAY

The open-plan office of a busy newspaper. Alex sits at his desk. He is talking on a telephone jammed against his shoulder and while he does so he is casually acknowledging and waving at colleagues.

ALEX

Now, was there a pet in the house? Yes, a pet, like a dog or budgie or a gerbil. You see, what I need is 'PC Plod rescues Harry the Hamster from House of Horror'. All right . . . well, that's a pity, you see, no pets, no human angle.

Alex hangs up.

INT. HUGO'S ROOM. DAY

Another view of the body: for example, from above.

INT. HOSPITAL. DAY

In the accident and emergency department of a busy hospital, Juliet sifts through a set of case notes. Another Doctor approaches her.

>   DOCTOR

Hi, there.

> *Juliet does not look up.*

>   JULIET

Hello.

>   DOCTOR

What happened to that guy?

>   JULIET

What guy?

>   DOCTOR

That guy, that one that died.

> *Juliet looks up.*

33

JULIET

What guy that died?

DOCTOR

That one, last week.

JULIET

Here?

DOCTOR

Yeah, here, I mean, where else?

JULIET

Oh, him. Well, he died.

DOCTOR
(*satisfied*)

That's what I thought.

INT. HUGO'S ROOM. DAY

The body, still present, exposed and motionless. The curtain flutters by the open window.

INT. LUMSDEN'S OFFICE. DAY

Lumsden, a middle-aged chartered accountant, is seated in a large chair behind a desk. He is talking to David, who appears distracted.

LUMSDEN

What do we do here, David?

DAVID

Sorry?

LUMSDEN

Here.

DAVID

Right here?

LUMSDEN

In this firm.

DAVID

Well, it's a wide range of, eh –

LUMSDEN

Accounting, David, chartered accounting –

DAVID

Exactly what I was –

LUMSDEN

– is often sneered at. Were you aware of that?

DAVID

Not any real sneering as such, no.

LUMSDEN

There's a whole wide world out there, and it all needs to be accounted for, doesn't it?

DAVID

Eh –

LUMSDEN

But they sneer, don't they?

DAVID

I'm not sure –

LUMSDEN

Oh, it's unfashionable, I know, but, yes, we're methodical, yes, we're diligent, yes, we're serious, and where's the crime in that, and why not shout it from the rooftops, yes, maybe sometimes we are a little bit boring, but by God, we get the job done.

DAVID

Yes, sir.

LUMSDEN

And that's why I think you fit in here.

DAVID

I'm boring?

LUMSDEN

You get the job done.

DAVID

Oh, I see, I thought you meant –

LUMSDEN

Which is why I'm trusting you with this account.

Lumsden throws a heavy folder into David's lap.

INT. HUGO'S ROOM. EVENING

It is almost dark. Only the familiar contour is visible through the gloom.

INT. STAIRWELL. EVENING

David ascends the stairs to the flat.

INT. LIVING ROOM. EVENING

Alex sits in an armchair facing out of the window. Juliet stands facing into the room. David, the last home, appears in the doorway.

DAVID

He's still here.

ALEX

He couldn't get his car started.

DAVID

When are you going to let the police know?

ALEX

You call them if you want.

DAVID
(to Juliet)

And what about you?

JULIET

Well, I'm getting used to having him around.

INT. HUGO'S ROOM. DAY

The corpse as before.

INT. ACCOUNTANTS' OFFICES. DAY

David sits at his desk, looking across the office.

Crouched over a large array of other desks, young men and women in suits are poring over folders and columned books. No one is speaking except in muted tones on the telephone.

David watches them. He looks to his left and to his right: on either side young men like him are toiling over accounts. He turns and looks behind him, where another array of accountants sit.

He turns back to his desk and opens the file he was previously given. He looks at the columns of records of profit, with a large total at the bottom.

When David looks up he sees Juliet seated beside his desk. She smiles and directs his gaze, with her own, to the surrounding scene.

INT. HUGO'S ROOM. EVENING

The body in silhouette.

> **DAVID**
> (*voice-over*)

OK. Let's do it.

INT. DIY STORE. DAY

*Inside a large, brightly lit DIY store with Muzak playing in the
background. We start with a tracking shot along an aisle stacked with
potentially vicious tools.*

ALEX
(voice-over)

All right, now listen. We have to dispose of that body in such a
way as to make it unidentifiable, so that even if it is found, then
it's never anything more than an unknown corpse. Burning,
dumping at sea and straightforward burial are all flawed either by
fingerprints or, more commonly, by dental records. This I have
learned. Now, what I suggest is that we bury him out in the forest,
but first of all we remove his hands and his feet, which we
incinerate. And his teeth, which we just remove. It's as simple as
that.

*As the tracking shot ends, we see David's head and shoulders as he
looks at something off picture. Suddenly a spring-loaded screwdriver
appears and is 'fired' so that the tip stops a few millimetres from his
face. David winces as we see that Alex is holding it.*

I always wondered what these were for.

*Alex places the screwdriver down on the shelf and walks across the
aisle to pick up a saw and a hammer.*

Now, this is what we need. And this.

*Alex hands the tools to David, who looks at them with disgust. Alex
walks on.*

Now what else?

DAVID

I don't know.

ALEX

A spade, we need a spade – I wish you would concentrate – we
need a spade if we're going to dig a pit.

DAVID

So who's going to do it?

ALEX

Dig the pit, I don't know.

DAVID

No, not that.

ALEX

Then what? Who's going to do what?

DAVID

You know what I'm talking about.

ALEX

Do I? What? What? What are you talking about?

DAVID

You know what. Who's going to do it?

ALEX

We all are, David, we're all going to do it. Each of us, you, me and Juliet, will do his or her bit. Is that fair enough?

DAVID

I can't do it.

ALEX

I don't hear this.

DAVID

I won't be able to do it.

ALEX

You're telling me you want out? Already? You're telling me you don't want the money? Hugo is going off. He smells. The flat smells. We can't wait any longer.

DAVID

I'm just telling you I can't cut him up.

Alex turns away in disgust.

EXT. LANE. NIGHT

Late at night, in a quiet lane at the back of the flat, a hired Ford Transit is parked.

INT. VAN. NIGHT

Inside the dimly lit van, Alex and Juliet are laying down plastic on the floor.

> JULIET

Who's going to do it?

> ALEX

I thought we all were.

> JULIET

I don't think I can.

> ALEX

But you're a doctor. You kill people every day.

> JULIET

I still don't want to. It's different.

> ALEX

And now you tell me.

INT. UNDER WATER/BATHROOM. NIGHT

A Man's face is being held under water. Bubbles escape from his mouth and his eyes bulge.

Tim hauls the Man's head out of the bath. His legs and arms are bound with cord. Andy sits on a chair, watching.

Tim ducks the Man's head under the water again.

The Man's face as before.

INT. HUGO'S ROOM. NIGHT

We see Hugo's face just before Alex, David and Juliet wrap him in a sheet and thick, black plastic. They wear masks over their noses. The smell is making them uncomfortable and irritable.

> DAVID

There's something I want to ask.

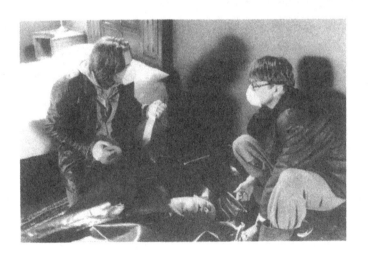

INT. BATHROOM. NIGHT

The Man's head has just been lifted from the water.

> MAN

I don't know. I swear to God, I don't know.

Tim ducks the Man's head back under the water.

INT. HUGO'S ROOM. NIGHT

> ALEX
> (*angry through his mask*)

Family? Family? Friends? Drugged-up wandering suicidal search of the self fuck-ups don't have families, David.

> DAVID

I just thought we sould discuss it.

> ALEX

Take his legs.

INT. STAIRWELL. NIGHT

In the stairwell of the flat, grunts of effort are heard as Alex, David and Juliet struggle with the heavy corpse, carrying it down the stairs wrapped in plastic sheeting. They come into view and go on down the stairs. They are all very tense and freeze with panic after accidentally banging against another flat's door. They swear at one another and continue their descent.

INT. BATHROOM. NIGHT

Tim is ducking the Man again. He writhes and struggles but is powerless to stop it.

EXT. BEHIND THE FLAT. NIGHT

The back yard and back door of the flats. The door opens and Alex, David and Juliet emerge, carrying the corpse out towards the van.

INT. LANDING OUTSIDE THE BATHROOM. NIGHT

From the landing we can see along the floor into the bathroom. The

Man's legs extend away from the bath. They are completely still. Andy and Tim stand beside them, looking down.

ANDY

You stupid bastard.

INT. VAN. NIGHT

Inside the back of the empty van. The door is opened and the body is half slid and half thrown inside. The door is closed and in the dark interior, the outline of the plastic lump is just visible, thanks to a streetlight. One of the doors opens again and David throws a bag of tools in. He then closes and locks the door.

INT. VAN. NIGHT

In the front of the van, David is climbing into the passenger side. Juliet and Alex are already in, with the latter at the wheel. Alex turns to the other two.

ALEX

Why don't we just draw lots for it?

The other two remain silent.

Whoever draws the short straw does it all. That way, you either do it or you don't. All or nothing.

JULIET

OK.

ALEX

David?

DAVID

I don't know.

ALEX

Look, if I draw the short straw, then I'll do it, but I'm not going to do it just because you won't.

Alex starts the engine of the van.

EXT. FOREST. NIGHT

Through the darkness we hear an engine, then the headlights of the van come into view.

It pulls off the track on to a patch of grass. The engine is switched off but the lights remain on. The trio descend from the van.

In front of the van, illuminated by its lights, Alex, David and Juliet stand together. Alex is showing them two long stems of grass and one short one. He encloses them in his fist and holds them out.

ALEX

All right, then, here we are and this is it. Do you want to play or not?

Alex holds his hand out towards Juliet, who takes the tip of one of the stems. It is one of the longer ones.

Alex and Juliet turn to David. Alex holds out the stems. David reaches out and takes one of the tips. It is the short straw.

DAVID

I can't do it.

EXT. FOREST. NIGHT

Deeper in the forest, with the headlamps still casting a little light through the trees, we see David's head and shoulders. His right arm is moving briskly back and forth accompanied by a vicious sawing noise. The sawing stops as he has evidently finished with one extremity. He shuffles back and starts sawing at another.

Alex leans against the spade in a shallow pit that he has dug. He observes David impassively. The sawing stops again.

DAVID

Finished.

ALEX

But not quite.

DAVID
(*hoping to distract Alex*)
Is that going to be deep enough?

Alex bends down to pick up the hammer, which he holds out towards David.

                    ALEX
Don't you worry about that.

                    JULIET
Is this necessary?

                    ALEX
Yes. Now come on, all or nothing.

Most reluctantly, David takes the hammer and looks at Alex, who gestures as if to say, 'On you go.' With revulsion on his face, he raises the hammer above his head.

INT. DAVID'S ROOM. DAY

David's face is visible against the plain white backdrop of his pillow.

He lies fully clothed on his bed, looking up at the ceiling. There is a knock at the door, then Juliet walks in.

                    JULIET
Are you all right?

                    DAVID
               (*without looking at Juliet*)
Oh, yes, I'm fine, thanks, just fine.

                    JULIET
Would you like to talk about it?

                    DAVID
No.

INT. LIVING ROOM. DAY

Alex sits with his feet up watching a noisy game show, while eating a snack and drinking from a can of beer. Newspapers lie scattered at his feet.

INT. LOFT. DAY

The loft above the flat is in darkness, but the trapdoor is opened, letting in a pool of light.

INT. HALL. DAY

David is pulling himself through the trapdoor up into the loft. Beneath him is a stepladder. Juliet stands half-way up the ladder, while Alex stands on the floor beside it. As David enters the loft, Alex hands up the bag of money to Juliet, who passes it on up to David.

JULIET

Be careful.

ALEX

Yeah, we don't want another stiff on our hands. Don't fall through the ceiling. OK? Is he listening to me?

JULIET

Stop nagging.

ALEX
(*to himself*)

I don't know why we couldn't stuff it in a mattress or put it under the floor like any normal human being. We could have hid it in the fridge.

INT. LOFT. DAY

David moves on into the dark cavernous loft, edging his way across beams and pipes. There are no skylights.

He stops and leans against some structure (the water tank). He strains to see in the darkness.

Suddenly there is a loud sucking and flowing noise as water empties from the water tank. David is startled and steps forward, tripping. He reaches out as he falls, striking a light switch. Briefly the loft is illuminated: David blinking as he lies across some beams, the large cavernous area, the pipes, the water tank, the bag of money lying between two rafters, and then the old brass switches begin to spark and the light goes out.

David scrambles towards the trapdoor.

INT. HUGO'S ROOM. DAY

Now cleaned and empty, with no trace of recent habitation.

INT. HOSPITAL. DAY

In a basement corridor in the hospital, pipes run along the ceiling. Above a fenced-off area is a sign saying 'For Incineration Only – No Aerosols'. On the floor of this area are yellow plastic sacks. Juliet appears around a corner carrying one of these. Quite casually she dumps it on the pile and continues past.

EXT. QUARRY. EVENING

Alex pushes a blue car into a quarry.

**[INT. SUBURBAN LOCK-UP GARAGE. NIGHT

In the garage there is a car, gardening equipment, several sacks of fertilizer and a trunk-style deep freeze, on the lid of which sit Andy and Tim. Tim takes out a cigarette and offers one to Andy, who declines.

They slide off the deep freeze and open it.

Inside the freezer there is a man, naked and bound with cord. They lift him up. He is very cold and weak.

The Man begins to whisper inaudibly. Andy moves his head so that he can hear the whisper. He listens, then nods approvingly.

They push him down again and close the lid. Andy holds the lid while Tim dumps the sacks of fertilizer on top.]

INT. CHARITY BALL. NIGHT

Alex, David and Juliet are attending a charity ball. Everyone is dressed very smartly, in ball gowns and black ties with the addition of a significant number in kilts.

Neither Alex nor David wears a kilt. The trio seem to know a number of people there but do not seem especially keen to speak to them.

A middle-aged, podgy, mustachioed Master of Ceremonies is standing on a platform in front of the band, making a speech to the diners who are still sat at their tables.

**Scene used later in final film.

MC

Ladies and gentlemen, may I have your attention please. First of all, may I thank you all for coming along tonight and supporting our appeal to raise funds for the sick children's unit.

There is a quick drum roll and applause breaks out. We move to the table where Alex, David and Juliet are seated. Alex leans across to Juliet.

ALEX

You didn't tell me that this was for children. I hate children. I'd raise money to have the little fuckers put down.

Some other guests around the table cast critical glances at Alex.

JULIET

Sshh.

ALEX

I want my money back. Excuse me.

Alex signals to the waiter by lifting his hand and snapping his fingers, then indicates another bottle of the champagne that already sits in front of him.

For all too often there's a complacency: out of sight, out of mind, let someone else bother about these things.

Alex cheers once and starts to applaud on his own. Juliet nudges him viciously.

But just before the dancing, I'd like to say a special thank-you to a few of the people who've worked so very hard to make this occasion actually happen.

The MC's drone continues in the background while conversation continues back at the table.

DAVID

Do you know many of these people?

JULIET

Yes. They're my friends.

ALEX

I see, so if they want to talk to you, we say you're not in.

MC

And now, ladies and gentlemen, and those of you who are neither or both –

Drum roll.

– would you make your way to the floor for the Strip the Willow.

JULIET

Are we going to dance?

ALEX

Well, it's physical contact, isn't it?

INT. DANCE FLOOR. NIGHT

The dance floor a few minutes later. It is packed and rather chaotic. Sweaty, dishevelled dancers sling one another around, with the thud of flesh against flesh. Toes are stood on and jackets discarded.

Juliet dances with Alex, who plunges in with the maximum of violence, eventually tripping up and tumbling forcefully among the other dancers.

He starts to get up, then rests his head back against the floor.

David has not been dancing. Instead he remains at their table and at the bar, drinking steadily and watching the other two.

INT. TABLE. NIGHT

Back at the table, while most people are still on the dance floor, the trio sit drinking and Alex smokes a cigar.

ALEX

That was good.

DAVID

Can we talk about something?

ALEX

Not now. I have an idea.

Alex pours champagne on to a stack of glasses.

DAVID

Listen, it's important. We need to talk about what we're going to do –

ALEX

Just stop worrying.

Alex stands and raises his glass.

Love and happiness for ever.

JULIET

For ever and ever.

Alex drinks, then puts his glass down. Juliet drinks but does not drain her glass. David sits still.

ALEX

What's the problem?

DAVID

I want to talk now.

ALEX

After you drink to love and happiness for ever.

DAVID

Now.

ALEX

After.

JULIET

David, I promise we will. Keep him happy.

ALEX

It's not for me, it's for love and happiness for ever.

David reaches out to take his glass. Suddenly Alex flings an arm out to point, knocking over David's glass and completely losing interest.

Look over there. It's Cameron.

JULIET

Who?

ALEX

Cameron. You remember Cameron.

JULIET

No, I don't.

ALEX

What's he doing here?

JULIET

That's not him.

ALEX

Yes, it is. It's him. Cameron, Cameron, come on over. Yo!

From some distance away, Cameron becomes aware of Alex and cautiously makes his way across until he stands a few feet from the table.

CAMERON

What?

ALEX

Nothing. We thought you were someone else.

Alex falls forwards, laughing, and the other two also laugh as Cameron walks away, humiliated again.

Good luck. I love that guy, but why does he have to follow us around?

DAVID

Anyway, what I was wanting to say was this –

BRIAN
(*unseen*)

The divine Juliet. Long time no see.

Brian has approached and is standing behind their table.

JULIET

Brian.

BRIAN

Would you care to dance?

DAVID

Hold on there. Who do you think you are?

BRIAN

What?

DAVID

Who do you think you are? You interrupted us.

BRIAN

I'm Brian McKinley, and who are you?

DAVID

Well, Brian McKinley, if you want to talk to my girlfriend, you talk to me first. If you want to dance with her, then you apply in writing three weeks in advance or you're gonna end up inside a fucking bin-bag. You didn't apply, so you don't dance.

Shocked and frightened, Brian backs away, then turns around to complete his departure. Juliet restrains David with a touch as they watch him go.

JULIET

Do you think you could try to be a little more forceful next time?

DAVID

I'm sorry.

JULIET

It's all right. I think he got the message anyway.

DAVID

That was quite stressful. I found that stressful.

ALEX

Yeah, but you were good, you were really good. 'Fucking bin-bag', I liked that. You were good. You explored your maleness to the full there.

DAVID

Do you think so?

JULIET

Well, you certainly had a good look around.

ALEX

You were magnificent.

INT. TOILETS. NIGHT

The gents' toilets. Brightly lit and white-tiled. Alex walks in and goes into a cubicle and closes the door. We hear him whistling and laughing as he passes urine. He keeps muttering 'bin-bag' to himself. Then he flushes the toilet and opens the door. As he does so a look of surprise appears on his face as he sees someone waiting for him.

ALEX

Cameron! What a surprise.

    As Alex is speaking Cameron's fist flies forward, hitting him in the face and sending him flying backwards. Cameron enters the cubicle and closes the door behind him.

INT. KITCHEN. MORNING

Juliet sits as before at the table. Alex sits opposite her, in his dressing gown. He looks vacant and unhappy, and there is bruising on his face. The newspapers are unread in a neat pile.

INT. HALL. MORNING

Mail falls through the letter box.

INT. KITCHEN. MORNING

Alex does not stir.

INT. HALL. MORNING

David emerges from his room, ready for work. He looks towards the kitchen, then walks to the door and opens it.

INT. KITCHEN. MORNING

We hear the main door closing as David leaves. Alex jolts with every sound. The telephone begins to ring. Juliet looks at Alex expectantly, but he does not move. Eventually she gets up and answers it.

JULIET

Hello. Hello.

ALEX

Who was it?

JULIET

Don't know. No one said anything.

ALEX

Rendered speechless with desire. I recall that feeling, from the days when I had such a thing.

JULIET

Are you all right?

ALEX

No.

JULIET

Then let's spend some money.

INT. FLAT. DAY

There follows a video depicting the results of Alex's and Juliet's spending spree. It opens with Alex seated at the kitchen table talking to the camera, absolutely deadpan.

ALEX

Hello. It's been a struggle, but now the days of worry are over, the light at the end of the tunnel has expanded into a golden sunrise and at last, at long last, nothing will ever be the same again.

Alex leans out and the camera follows him as he presses the play button on a tape recorder. The music begins.

Fast cuts follow, occasionally interrupted by out-of-focus shots of the floor or ceiling as the camera swivels round and is switched on and off.

Alex wearing several different suits, outfits and silk pyjamas.

Juliet wearing several different outfits.

Both of them posing with small objets d'art.

The expensive watch on Alex's wrist.

Juliet's jewellery.

Expensive toys.

Juliet takes a picture of Alex with a Polaroid camera.

Alex holds the camcorder out at arm's length in order to film himself and turns to the camera and adjusts his tie.

This is Alex Law reporting from the scene of his own life, and you know, I'm so happy I could die.

Darkness. TV. Turned off.

INT. LIVING ROOM. DAY

The music has stopped.

David presses the eject button and lifts the video from the player.

Alex and Juliet are seated on the sofa, surrounded by their acquisitions, and are evidently a little embarrassed. Juliet is holding the Polaroid of Alex.

DAVID
I think we ought to scrub this, don't you?

David reinserts the tape and presses record.

ALEX
Will you calm down.

JULIET
Yeah, you're making us all nervous.

David picks up the Polaroid of Alex and throws it down, then picks up a vase.

DAVID
How much did you pay for this?

ALEX
I don't know.

DAVID
How much did you pay?

ALEX
I don't know.

DAVID
How much?

ALEX
I don't know.

JULIET
Two hundred.

DAVID
Two hundred pounds?

JULIET
Two hundred pounds.

DAVID
You paid two hundred pounds for this?

JULIET
That's what it cost, David.

DAVID
No, no, no. That's what you paid for it. Two hundred pounds is what you paid for it. We don't know what it cost us yet, for you two to have a good time, we don't know the cost of that yet.

From out in the hall, the telephone starts to ring. Nobody moves.

INT. DAVID'S ROOM. NIGHT

David lies awake in his bed.

INT. A FLAT HALLWAY. NIGHT

In a dark hallway, a door is kicked forcefully open.

INT. DAVID'S ROOM. NIGHT

Hearing the noise, David sits up in bed, then gets out, reaching for his clothes.

INT. STAIRWELL. NIGHT

David looks down the stairwell. Other neighbours, in nightclothes or hurriedly dressed, are standing at the open door of the flat below. David descends the stairs and looks into the hall of the other flat where the occupant, an Elderly Woman, lies groaning on the floor.

A hand on David's shoulder pushes him out of the way and two uniformed policemen walk past, followed by ambulance men carrying a stretcher.

DAVID

Did they take anything? Did they take anything?

No one acknowledges his question or answers it.

The ambulance men emerge carrying the woman, her face bruised and cut. Everyone else begins to melt away.

INT. STAIRWELL. NIGHT

David stands alone on the darkened stairwell.

INT. DAVID'S ROOM. NIGHT

David lies awake in his bed.

*[INT. DOOR OF THE FLAT. DAY

Someone attempts to open the door but cannot because there are two new security chains on the inside. The door is forced against the chains with no success and Alex calls out from the other side.

ALEX

What is this? What is going on? David!

David approaches the door.

DAVID

I'll let you in.

David closes the door and looks through a new spyhole to see Alex grinning at him while he releases the chains and then opens the door again. Alex walks in.

ALEX

What is this?

DAVID

Security.

ALEX

For what? Jehovah's Witnesses?

DAVID

There was a break-in.

ALEX

Downstairs, I know. Pensioner's terror ordeal: page six.

Alex hands David a rolled-up newspaper.

DAVID

Doesn't it worry you?

ALEX

No, it doesn't. I've tried to let it worry me but it won't. I've worked on that paper for three years. There is a pensioner's terror ordeal on page six every day. Every day. Maybe when I'm a pensioner it'll worry me.

*Cut from completed film.

Alex notices some more tools and the stepladder leading up to the trapdoor.

What's all this for, more security?

DAVID

I fitted a lock up there. On the inside.

ALEX

Oh, that'll come in useful.]

INT. KITCHEN. NIGHT

Alex is serving on to plates from a large bowl of pasta.

David and Juliet sit at the table.

*[JULIET
Is this the same stuff you made last week?

ALEX

No, no, it's different.

JULIET

I hope it tastes better than the other stuff.

ALEX

It tastes different.

JULIET

I don't want it to taste different. I don't know why I bother.] Is that enough for you? Hey!

DAVID

What? Yes, that's fine.

ALEX

You're sure? There's lots more.

DAVID

No, I'm sure, that'll be enough.

ALEX

What's wrong?

*Cut from completed film.

DAVID

Nothing.

ALEX

You're not eating.

DAVID

Not eating what?

ALEX

Not eating like you used to, that's what.

DAVID

If you give me the plate, I'll eat.

Alex hands him the plate and he starts to eat. Alex watches him chew a mouthful.

ALEX

Now swallow.

David does so.

You know, you should spend some of that money instead of worrying about it. That's my advice.

JULIET

He's right. You'd feel much better about it all.

David has stopped eating.

ALEX

Once it's spent you won't have to worry about it.

JULIET

Be like a weight off your shoulders.

ALEX

You know we're right.

JULIET

Don't you?

DAVID

I want to secure it.

Secure it? What do you mean – you're going to take it to a bank? You're not going to take it to a bank? You're not going to take it to a bank? Or what, you want to bury it? Is that it?

JULIET

I don't see the point in that.

ALEX

Because that's no good. Remember, we did what we did, we took the money. It was a material calculation. But what's the use if it's underground, or in some funny bank in some funny place? If you can't spend it, if you can't have it, what use is it? None. It's nothing, all for nothing, if you do that. I didn't get into this for nothing, so that I could have nothing –

DAVID

Yeah, and you didn't saw his feet off.

There is silence. David resumes eating.

It tastes different.

INT. HALL. NIGHT.

The trapdoor is closed and we hear the lock turning.

INT. KITCHEN. NIGHT.

Alex stands at the sink doing some washing up. He hears footsteps from the loft above. He stops what he is doing and walks slowly out to the hall.

INT. LOFT. NIGHT

In the darkness we can just make out David's eyes as he sits in silence.

ALEX
(*calling from below*)
David, David, what are you doing up there?

The torch goes on. David lifts the bag of money from between the rafters. He puts it inside another thick yellow plastic bag, which he ties tightly with string.

> *David then opens the water tank.*
>
> *Alex's voice can be heard throughout.*

>> (*calling from below*)

Will you come down now. It's not safe up there. Are you listening to me? Security and insanity are not the same thing.

INT. HALL. NIGHT

>> ALEX

Shit.

*[INT. KITCHEN. MORNING

Juliet sits drinking coffee, while Alex stands in the doorway looking up towards the trapdoor.

>> JULIET

Leave him alone.

>> ALEX

He can't stay up there.

>> JULIET

He'll come down. Just leave him alone.

>> ALEX

Yeah, he's got to go to work, hasn't he? You think he'll come down for that?

>> JULIET

No, but he's looking after the money, so what's the problem?

>> ALEX

Looking after it – he's probably fucking well eating it.]

*[INT. HOSPITAL. DAY

Juliet looks through the door from a small office out into the main waiting area in the casualty department. It is busy and there are rows of people nursing injuries waiting to be seen. More file past the door while she watches with no enthusiasm.]

*Cut from completed film.

64

INT. HALL. DAY

The trapdoor opens. David's head appears. He looks around and listens carefully.

INT. LUMSDEN'S OFFICE. DAY

Lumsden answers his telephone.

INT. HALL. DAY

David speaks on the telephone.

> DAVID
>
> It's my mother, sir, she's very ill and I think I need to be with her just now. I don't know. The doctors aren't sure. It could go either way. Yes, sir, I'll certainly stay in touch.

INT. BATHROOM. DAY

David shaves carefully with a safety razor.

*[INT. KITCHEN. DAY

Bacon and eggs fry in a pan. David attends to them while drinking from a large tumbler of orange juice.

INT. HOSPITAL. DAY

A Sister hands Juliet a casualty case sheet. Juliet reads it.

> JULIET
>
> Painful groin? What does that mean?

> SISTER
>
> I don't know. He wouldn't show me.]

Juliet draws back the curtain of a cubicle. Alex is sitting on a trolley.

*[
> ALEX
>
> Boy, am I glad to see you.

*Cut from completed film.

JULIET

What are you doing here?

ALEX

We have to talk.

JULIET

Your painful groin?

She turns and walks away. Alex chases after her.

ALEX

Later. But first – him.]

JULIET

David?

ALEX

Exactly. Now I've been thinking –

JULIET

Oh, good.

ALEX

He won't do anything for me, but for you –

JULIET

Forget it.

ALEX

He isn't safe up there. If you really cared about him, you'd use
your influence to get him down, then he'd be safe.

JULIET

And the money?

ALEX

We could put it somewhere.

JULIET

Where he can't get it?

ALEX

Now you thought of that, not me.

JULIET

Forget it – he'll come down.

Juliet walks away.

INT. HALL. DAY

The hall is empty and the flat is silent. We see the trapdoor.

INT. LOFT. EVENING

David sits in the darkness. A crack of light penetrates beside the trapdoor.

INT. KITCHEN. NIGHT

Alex and Juliet sit at the table, eating in silence.

The doorbell rings. Alex and Juliet look at one another.

ALEX

Expecting anyone?

JULIET

No.

ALEX

Oh.

Alex resumes eating.

JULIET

Aren't you going to answer it?

ALEX

Well, I'm not expecting anyone either.

Juliet glares at him.

INT. HALL. NIGHT

Alex approaches the door and is about to open it. At the last moment he checks himself and looks through the spyhole.

INT. THROUGH THE SPYHOLE. NIGHT

Tim and Andy stand outside the door.

INT. HALL. NIGHT

Alex, slightly puzzled, fixes the security chains before opening the door. As soon as he opens it, the door is kicked wide open as the security chains break off. Tim and Andy enter the flat.

In a whirlwind of force they drag and shove Alex and Juliet into the living room and bind them up with cord. There are no words apart from swiftly muffled cries.

At the end of this Andy stands in front of Alex holding a crowbar. Swiftly and without warning, he cracks it across Alex's shins. Then Andy slowly puts one end of the crowbar into Alex's mouth. For a moment he does nothing, then just as slowly again, he takes the crowbar out.

ALEX

It's in the loft.

INT. HALL. NIGHT

The trapdoor is closed but the sound of it being unlocked can just be heard (although not by anyone in the flat).

INT. HALL. NIGHT

Tim pulls the ladder across to the trapdoor.

INT. LOFT. NIGHT

It is completely dark in the loft, but as the trapdoor opens a shaft of light strikes upwards and illuminates a small pool around the opening.

INT. LOFT. NIGHT

Away from the trapdoor there appears to be a wall of uniform darkness, but then we see a pair of eyes in the darkness. It is David. He stands perfectly still.

There is a hammer in his right hand.

INT. LOFT. NIGHT

Tim's head appears through the trapdoor. Cautiously he lifts himself through and balances on the beams.

INT. HALL. NIGHT

The hall is empty, but we can see the open trapdoor. Suddenly there is a single thud, as might be caused by a body landing heavily on and across some beams in the loft.

INT. LOFT. NIGHT

David stands motionless in the dark, exactly as before.

INT. LIVING ROOM. NIGHT

Andy has heard the single thud. He strains to hear anything else but does not. Slowly he backs away to the door of the living room, keeping the crowbar trained on Alex as he does so. He looks back and up towards the trapdoor.

INT. LOFT. NIGHT

Once again a small pool of light emanates from the open trapdoor. Andy emerges into this, crowbar in hand, peering into the darkness. Carefully he stands up and moves out of the light and steps across the beams. His foot strikes something and he looks down. Tim's body lies spread-eagled beneath him. He looks up. To one side of him is the brass light switch. Andy lifts his arm, reaches towards it and switches it on. Sparks pour out for a moment and then the light comes on for a fraction of a second, long enough for Andy to see David's face is only centimetres from his own.

INT. HALL. NIGHT

Alex and Juliet are bound together as before. There is a loud thud from the ceiling, followed by a few heavy steps. Then Andy's body falls headfirst through the trapdoor, straight down to the floor below, landing awkwardly and coming to rest with his head hanging back, looking towards Alex and Juliet. Andy takes one agonal breath and dies. Blood trickles from the side of his mouth.

Tim's body lands on Andy.

David drops himself from the hatch to the floor.

David takes a large knife from a wooden block.

Back in the hall he kneels, holding the knife, beside Tim. Noticing something at the top of Tim's neck, he uses the knife to lift away Tim's T-shirt. A tattoo covers Tim's neck. David looks at it, then stands up.

He walks through to the living room, where Alex and Juliet, still bound, watch him approach. He looks at them for a moment, then extends the knife and cuts the cord in one place.

EXT. FOREST. NIGHT

In a scene similar to the dismemberment of Hugo, we see David's shoulders as he saws back and forth at something unseen. He stops and reaches out for the hammer, picks it up and raises it above his head.

EXT. ROAD. DAWN

The van is silhouetted against a rising sun.

INT. BACK OF THE VAN. DAWN

The tools and the yellow sack slide about in the back of the van.

INT. VAN. DAWN

David is driving. Alex and Juliet are huddled silently away from him. David seems quite at ease.

A thick bunch of keys dangles from the ignition. Juliet observes them.

INT. LOFT. DAY

David sits still in the darkness.

*[INT. NEWSPAPER OFFICE. DAY

Alex sits at his desk fidgeting, about to write something but unable to start. On the screen of his word processor is a page mock-up with the

*Cut from completed film.

headline 'CATS EAT PENSIONER'. As the telephone on his desk rings, he is startled, then reaches out, slowly lifts it fractionally and replaces it.]

INT. TRAVEL AGENT'S. DAY

Hunched over a VDU, the Salesman is offering Juliet a range of flights.

SALESMAN
October 15th, direct flight, London Heathrow to Rio de Janeiro, British Airways, you are looking at seven hundred and sixty-five pounds. Seven six five.

JULIET
That sounds fine.

SALESMAN
Air Portugal, on the other hand, via Lisbon, same day, five hundred and sixty-five. Five six five. It's up to you. Catering important?

JULIET
What?

SALESMAN
Air France. Glasgow. Direct, but then you're looking at the wrong end of nine hundred and twelve pounds. That's nine one two. It's up to you.

JULIET
Yes, the first one's fine. Heathrow direct.

SALESMAN
It's up to you. Air Patagonia. New outfit: via Caracas and Bogotá. No catering. Four hundred and eleven pounds. Four one one. Good value, but refuelling at Bogotá is variable.

JULIET
The first one was fine.

SALESMAN
Well, it's up to you. Seven six five. How will you be paying?

INT. HALL. NIGHT

The hall is empty but we can hear David's footsteps on the beams above.

INT. LIVING ROOM. NIGHT

Alex sits watching The Wicker Man *on television. He can hear the footsteps above. He turns the sound up on the television so that he cannot hear them, but he keeps looking up to the ceiling, as though he expects to hear them or to see something.*

Eventually he turns the sound back down and, after a moment's silence, the footsteps start again, back and forth, then stop.

Alex looks up.

Without warning there is the sound of an electric drill.

The blade of the drill appears through the ceiling and is then withdrawn. Alex is shocked. Other drill holes appear.

INT. VARIOUS CEILINGS. NIGHT

Holes are drilled in the ceilings.

INT. LOFT. NIGHT

Rods of light penetrate up from the holes, interrupting but not obliterating the darkness. David sits back, pleased with his work.

INT. JULIET'S ROOM. NIGHT

Juliet sits at her desk. Alex stands in the doorway. He is about to speak. Juliet raises a finger to her lips. They both look at the ceiling.

EXT. GARDEN AT FRONT OF THE FLAT. NIGHT

Establishing shot of Alex and Juliet in garden.

INT. HALL. NIGHT

The trapdoor is open.

INT. ALEX'S ROOM. NIGHT

David is searching through Alex's desk, looking through letters and folders, then shoving them back into drawers.

EXT. GARDEN AT FRONT OF THE FLAT. NIGHT

                    ALEX
No, definitely not. And that's that. I refuse to discuss it further.

                    JULIET
It's the only way.

                    ALEX
I refuse.

                    JULIET
You're frightened.

                    ALEX
No, I'm not frightened. A little terrified maybe. Did you see what happened to the last two who tried that. They went up alive and they came down dead – the difference, I mean, alive dead dead alive, that sort of thing. It wasn't difficult to spot. He killed them both: he cut them up.

INT. JULIET'S ROOM. NIGHT

David is now searching through Juliet's desk. He picks up a large brown envelope and looks into it. Beneath it is the airline ticket envelope.

The doorbell rings.

INT. THROUGH THE SPYHOLE. NIGHT

McCall and Mitchell stand outside the door.

INT. HALL. NIGHT

David opens the door. McCall smiles.

MCCALL

Good evening. I'm Detective Inspector McCall and this is DC Mitchell. I wonder if we could ask you some questions.

DAVID

What about?

MCCALL

It's about the burglary.

DAVID

Burglary?

MCCALL

Downstairs.

DAVID

Of course.

MCCALL

Can we come in?

INT. LIVING ROOM. NIGHT

David sits on the sofa while the two policemen sit on armchairs several feet apart.

DAVID

So I just heard her cries for help and all that, and when I went downstairs there were already those other people there, so I just stood around really, waiting – you know how people do – and then when your colleagues arrived I came back upstairs. And that's about all, I think. I didn't actually see anything useful, I don't think.

MCCALL

Did you hear anything before her cries?

DAVID

No, not that I recall. I was asleep.

MCCALL

Have you seen anything or anyone suspicious around here in the last few days?

DAVID

No, nothing, sorry.

MCCALL

Well, if you do, you'll let us know?

DAVID

Of course.

MCCALL

And the other three people in the flat, did they hear anything?

DAVID

There are only two other people in the flat.

McCall consults a notebook.

MCCALL

Two?

DAVID

Who said there were four?

MCCALL

We understood there were four people living here. Not always, of course, but now, four.

DAVID

No, three. Who said there were four?

MCCALL

How strange. And how unsatisfactory to have misleading information. Only three people here. You're sure?

DAVID

Yes, absolutely.

MCCALL

Take a note of that, Mitchell. Only three, rather than four. Write it down. You can use numbers or words, I have no preference. Which are you using?

MITCHELL

Both, sir.

MCCALL

Excellent. DC Mitchell is a rising star, Mr Stevens. Under my tutelage he will undoubtedly make the grade.

DAVID

I see.

MCCALL

I doubt it. *[And these other two people, did they hear anything?

DAVID

No, they were asleep. They didn't even wake up.

MCCALL

Yes. Why do you think you woke and they didn't?

DAVID

I don't know. Maybe I'm a lighter sleeper.]

Uncomfortably, David realizes that Mitchell has noted down even this last, trivial remark in a painful longhand and has underlined a short segment of it.

*[INT. HALL. NIGHT

In the hallway of the flat Mitchell stands at the open main door, waiting to leave. McCall is kneeling at the door to Hugo's room, tracing his finger down the broken lintel and lock. David looks on.

MCCALL

Looks like you had a break-in up here as well.

DAVID

Someone lost the key.

McCall gently pushes the door open and the light from the hall illuminates Hugo's room.

MCCALL

Is this where no one stays?

DAVID

Yeah, that's right, that's it.

*Cut from completed film.

78

David notices that Mitchell is writing this down.]

EXT. GARDEN AT FRONT OF THE FLAT. NIGHT

ALEX

You'll wait in the hall?

JULIET

I'll wait there.

ALEX

And if it sounds like I'm being killed, you'll phone the police,
you'll tell them everything?

JULIET

Everything.

ALEX

Everything. Except maybe it was his idea and not mine in the first
place. OK? That's important to me. I need to die misunderstood.

JULIET

Alex.

ALEX

What?

JULIET

As smart as you are, you'll need a little help.

She hands Alex a Yale key. Alex stares at it.

INT. LOFT. NIGHT

In the darkness, the sound of the lock being turned is heard.

INT. HALL. NIGHT

Alex stands at the top of the ladder, holding the key in the trapdoor lock.

ALEX

All right, David, what I'm going to do is, I'm going to open this
lock and I'm going to come up, and what's important is that you
remain calm.

There is one light on. Juliet stands at the bottom of the ladder. Having opened the trapdoor, Alex stops and listens, but there is no sound above his own breathing. Juliet throws up a torch, which he catches. He switches it on. It shines, then goes out, and he knocks it against the ladder, making it work again. Slowly he pushes the trapdoor open.

INT. LOFT. NIGHT

The trapdoor opens. Below it, Alex crouches on the ladder, expecting attack at any moment. He looks back down to Juliet, who returns his gaze, then slowly he raises himself into the loft.

He turns around quickly, darting the torchlight around into corners and squinting in the darkness, but he sees nothing.

The torch goes out. Cursing, he knocks it against a beam and it shines again.

Slowly he moves further from the trapdoor into the centre of the loft, still turning around and worried about what might be behind or above him.

INT. HALL. NIGHT

Juliet stands waiting, braced for sound of conflict.

INT. LOFT. NIGHT

Alex is still looking but has relaxed a little, feeling less in danger. In one corner he notices David's pile of loft-possessions and the mat on which he has been sleeping. He moves towards it.

INT. HALL. NIGHT

Juliet stands, still waiting.

INT. LOFT. NIGHT

Alex stands in David's corner. With another sweep of the torch he can still see nothing. He calls to Juliet.

ALEX

He isn't up here.

INT. HALL. NIGHT

A close-up of Juliet's face, just as David's hand slams across her mouth, gripping her tightly while his other hand clamps the back of her head. David's mouth is right up against her ear as he spits a warning into it.

DAVID

Tell him to look for the money.

Slowly, David relaxes his grip on Juliet.

JULIET

Look for the money.

INT. LOFT. NIGHT

Alex, quite cheerful now, is looking in the rafters.

ALEX

Don't worry. That's what I'm doing.

INT. HALL. NIGHT

David holds Juliet across her face again. She is terrified and does not struggle.

*[DAVID

Expecting anyone?

JULIET

What?

DAVID

Were you expecting anyone? Tonight?

JULIET

No.

DAVID

Visitors? Some friends maybe? Someone you talked to?

*Cut from completed film.

81

                              JULIET

No one. I promise.

                               DAVID

Who have you talked to?

                              JULIET

No one.

                               DAVID

If I think you're lying –]

INT. LOFT. NIGHT

Alex stands gazing around the loft.

                               ALEX
                          (from the loft)

Well, it's not up here.

INT. HALL. NIGHT

David pulls Juliet to one side.

INT. LOFT. NIGHT

Alex is about to descend when he notices the water tank. He walks over and lifts the lid. His face breaks into a smile as he realizes what it holds. He dips an arm into the tank, raises the yellow bag, then quickly lowers it again. Alex steps back from the water tank.

INT. HALL. NIGHT

Alex appears at the top of the ladder. Without looking, he slides down as quickly as he can, calling out as he does so.

                               ALEX

Juliet, I have –

   Alex reaches the base of the ladder. He turns around to find himself facing the blade of the battery-operated drill, held by David. Juliet stands off to one side.

– a problem.

David holds the drill even closer until it is almost touching the centre of Alex's forehead and presses the 'trigger' to turn the blade slowly as he speaks.

Alex does not move at all.

DAVID

You looking for me?

ALEX

Looking for you? Yes.

DAVID

What for? What did you want? The money? Was that it?

ALEX

We just wanted to speak to you.

Alex's hands and sleeves are wet. A few drops of water fall from his fingertips. Unnoticed by the other two, he slowly wipes his hands on the back of his jeans.

DAVID

Who else have you just wanted to speak to? Maybe you thought they'd already got me.

The blade of the drill scrapes Alex's skin.

ALEX

Who?

DAVID

Your friends.

ALEX

I don't know what you're talking about.

JULIET

He doesn't know David.

David holds the drill back slightly while he thinks. It could go either way.

DAVID

Well, maybe you don't –

David lowers the drill and smiles.

I'm talking about the police.

INT. ALEX'S ROOM. DAY

Alex has just woken up. He rubs at his forehead. There is a nick in it, where the drill scratched. He rubs at it and examines the drop of blood on the end of his finger.

INT. DAVID'S POINT OF VIEW. ALEX'S ROOM. DAY

Looking down from a hole in the ceiling, we see into Alex's room, where he is getting dressed. As he finishes dressing he leaves his room.

INT. HALL. DAY

Alex leaves his room and enters the hall.

INT. LOFT. DAY

David scurries across the beams to look down through a hole above the hall.

INT. LOFT/HALL. DAY

Looking down on Alex as he leaves the flat and closes the door.

INT. LOFT. DAY

David scurries back across the beams to look down through another hole. He looks for several seconds.

NOTE *In the following sequence, Juliet's face is not seen until her comment on it.*

INT. JULIET'S ROOM. DAY

Juliet lies on her bed. She throws the covers back.

INT. LOFT. DAY.

David is still looking down through the hole.

84

INT. JULIET'S ROOM. DAY

Juliet moves around her room. She is wearing a large, baggy T-shirt.

INT. LOFT. DAY

David still watching.

INT. JULIET'S ROOM. DAY

Juliet's legs are seen as the T-shirt lands on the floor beside them.

INT. LOFT. DAY

David sits back suddenly, recoiling from this activity. He scrambles back across to his mat, where he sits back down and closes his eyes. Then he opens them and scrambles back to look down again.

INT. JULIET'S ROOM. DAY

The room is empty

The sound of the flat door closing is heard.

From David's point of view we see:

   INT. LOFT/HALL (EMPTY). DAY

   INT. LOFT/LIVING ROOM (EMPTY). DAY

   INT. LOFT/KITCHEN (EMPTY). DAY

INT. HALL. DAY

David's head appears beneath the trapdoor. He hangs from the hatch and drops down to the floor.

INT. BATHROOM. DAY

David showers.

INT. HALL. DAY

David emerges from the bathroom and walks towards the kitchen. We follow him in.

INT. KITCHEN. DAY

David takes orange juice out of the fridge and pours himself a glass. He sits at the table and looks briefly into a corner that we cannot see. The expression on his face does not change and his voice is impassive.

                    DAVID
I thought you'd gone to work.

                    JULIET
                   (unseen)
With a face like this?

INT. KITCHEN. DAY

Juliet's face. There are bruises across it where she was gripped by David.

INT. MONITOR SCREEN/NEWSPAPER OFFICE. DAY

In close-up we track along the following half-sentence: 'In the event of my death I want the following facts to be known: –'

The remainder of the screen is blank.

Alex sits at his desk, deciding what to type next on to the screen seen before. A young Office Boy approaches his desk.

                    BOY
The editor wants to see you.

INT. KITCHEN. DAY

David sits still while Juliet talks. She is now seated just behind him.

*[JULIET
I remember how things used to be here, and I see how they are now, and I don't know why it is. I don't know how we let you become like this. We were your friends and we should have looked after you.]

*Cut from completed film.

86

INT. EDITOR'S OFFICE. DAY

Alex sits nervously while the Editor sits on the side of his desk.

EDITOR

Out in the woods. Three bodies. Decomposed. Mutilated. Beyond recognition.

ALEX

I don't know anything about it.

EDITOR

Of course you don't know anything about it. If you knew anything about it, I wouldn't have to send you out there to cover it.

ALEX

Cover it?

EDITOR

That's right. This is your break.

ALEX

Cover it?

EDITOR

Well?

*[ALEX

But there's no –

EDITOR

Animals involved? I know, but you need a change. And besides, we're short.]

ALEX

I don't know.

EDITOR

Don't know what?

ALEX

Well, I've got this story, it's really good, I'm working on, that is good, I feel it could be big, it's this, eh, and it's, you know, it's incredible. Am I right, you did say 'beyond recognition'?

*Cut from completed film.

87

INT. KITCHEN. DAY

David and Juliet are seated as before.

DAVID

I'm sorry.

JULIET

I should hope so.

David turns towards her. He reaches out and softly touches her face.

DAVID

Maybe we can still sort everything out.

Juliet takes his hand.

JULIET

Well, we could always try.

They look at one another.

EXT. FOREST. DAY

Several police and unmarked vehicles, including one mobile 'incident room', stand on a rough track. Another car arrives at the end and is parked to one side. Alex steps out.

From where he stands, Alex can see towards the site of the burials. There are a few policemen, uniformed and plain-clothes, and a small knot of journalists, kept at bay by plastic tape draped from tree to tree. Mounds of earth mark the site of the exhumations.

Alex walks past the other journalists into the woods. He looks back towards the sight, then turns to look in the opposite direction. He finds himself at the edge of a golf course. From the green to the graves is hardly any distance.

To one side, Alex sees McCall and Mitchell, hunched in earnest discussion. Mitchell looks up briefly and catches Alex's eye.

INT. KITCHEN/HALL. DAY

The kitchen is empty. We track through the kitchen and out into the hall, stopping at the door to Juliet's room.

INT. JULIET'S ROOM. DAY

David and Juliet are seated on the bed. Among the junk on her be table is the Polaroid photograph of Alex, propped up against a tumbler. Juliet reaches out and turns it away before pulling Davia towards her.

INT. MOBILE INCIDENT ROOM. DAY

Several journalists sit close together on plastic chairs. Alex sits at t back, near the half-open door. At the other end, three police office them. They are a medium-ranking Uniformed Officer, and to one of him Mitchell and then McCall, both of whom sit in silence.

UNIFORMED OFFICER

All right, ladies and gentlemen, the releasable and print-wort facts of the day so far are as follows. Late yesterday afternoor forestry workers came across one set of human remains lying grave which appeared to have been recently dug. Further excavation on our part has revealed two similar, deeper grave again containing human remains.

Alex turns his head and looks out of the door towards the buria now enclosed in a plastic tent. He continues to stare at it.

While Alex is looking, the sound of laughter and Uniformed Oj subsequent comments become muted and we hear the memory o; sound in Alex's head: it is the noise of the saw going back and j across the victim's limbs.

As and when the corpses are removed, we will endeavour to ascertain the mode of death and duration of burial, as well a: identification, which will of course be passed on to you after informing, where possible, the next of kin.

Alex discreetly stands up and slips out of the van.

EXT. FOREST. DAY

As he reaches his car, Alex fumbles in his pockets for his keys. He is sweating and trembling. He drops his keys. As he bends down to pick them up, his foot slips on the wet grass. He falls to his knees, his forehead banging against the car door. He kneels for a moment, gripping the keys, his head resting against the door.

The noise of the sawing stops.

From behind, the arm of a Police Constable reaches out and his hand rests on Alex's shoulder.

Alex turns around to see the Constable looming over him.

CONSTABLE

Are you all right sir?

INT. MOBILE INCIDENT ROOM. DAY

The Uniformed Officer continues.

McCall is staring impassively at the empty chair by the door.

INT. ALEX'S CAR. DAY

Alex sits in his car, staring ahead. Eventually he puts the key in the ignition.

EXT. STREET. NIGHT

The outside of the tenement.

INT. STAIRWELL. NIGHT

Alex ascends the stairs. He is carrying three copies of the next day's edition.

INT. HALL. NIGHT

Alex enters the flat. The hall is dark but light comes from the living room. He moves towards it.

INT. LIVING ROOM. NIGHT

Alex opens the door. Juliet sits with her back to him, while David looks out of the window. Concerned for Juliet, Alex approaches her.

ALEX

Are you all right?

JULIET

Yes, of course. Why wouldn't I be?

Rebuffed, Alex takes in the situation.

ALEX

I don't know. I thought maybe I was –

JULIET

We were just sorting things out.

She and David exchange a glance.

ALEX

Well, you'd better read all about it.

Alex drops the newspapers on the table in front of Juliet.

The headline reads 'TRIPLE CORPSE HORROR'.

DAVID

We already know. All about it.

JULIET

It was on the television.

Alex picks up the papers.

ALEX
(*nervously*)

Of course, but I think you'll find the print medium provides a
more lucid and detailed –

JULIET

Oh, shut up, Alex.

DAVID

It wasn't deep enough. I told you it wasn't deep enough, but you
wouldn't listen.

It doesn't necessarily matter. They don't even know who those people are, and even if they did, they have nothing to connect them with us, nothing at all.

DAVID

I'm glad that you're so certain, Alex. It makes us feel a whole lot better.

ALEX

I beg your pardon?

JULIET

It makes us feel a whole lot better.

ALEX

That's what I thought he said.

INT. ALEX'S ROOM. NIGHT

Alex lies asleep. Slow track towards him.

INT. KITCHEN. DAY. DREAM

McCall and Mitchell are standing in the centre of the kitchen. They say nothing. Mitchell leans down and begins to poke at the slender gap between two floorboards as though trying to get his finger into it. This appears impossible but he manages nevertheless. His finger digs in, while McCall watches. Gradually Mitchell takes a grip of the floorboard. It is nailed down fast and Mitchell strains as he pulls. Eventually the nails fly out and, in a flurry of cracks and splinters, the plank comes away.

McCall and Mitchell look down. In the gap between the rafters, Alex is lying face down and trying to crawl away under the floorboards.

Mitchell grabs Alex's ankle and McCall is now holding a saw.

INT. ALEX'S ROOM. NIGHT

Alex awakens abruptly and in shock. He is sweating. Just as he recovers his composure, he sees a form, almost hidden in the darkness, sitting on the end of his bed.

ALEX

Who the fuck?

He braces himself for a fight and fumbles at the bedside light switch.

JULIET

Sshh. Stop.

Alex leaves the light off.

ALEX

What are you doing here?

Juliet pauses.

JULIET

It's about me and David.

ALEX

The perfect couple, I should say.

JULIET

You mustn't take it so badly.

ALEX

Don't worry about it. I'd do exactly the same, but I don't think I'm his type.

JULIET

Don't you ever stop?

ALEX

No.

Alex slumps back, eyes closed, asleep almost instantly.

Juliet watches him.

INT. LIVING ROOM. DAY

McCall and Mitchell sit opposite Juliet, who is being questioned. They watch her while she studies photographs of Hugo, Tim and Andy intently. Eventually, McCall breaks the silence. Mitchell takes notes continuously.

MCCALL

Take all the time you like, doctor.

JULIET

I'm sorry, I've never seen any of them.

MCCALL

Look again if you like.

Juliet glances at the photographs.

JULIET

No. I haven't seen them.

MCCALL

Do you think you have a good memory for faces?

JULIET

Same as everyone else.

MCCALL

But in your work you must meet lots of different people, every day – new people, new faces. No?

JULIET

Yes.

MCCALL

And what do you recognize, names or faces?

JULIET

Diseases.

MCCALL

Like recognizing criminals by their crimes.

JULIET

I suppose so.

MCCALL

I mean, that's what it's like.

JULIET

Sorry?

MCCALL

And you said you supposed so, but I wasn't offering it for debate.

MITCHELL

Offering it for debate.

MCCALL

It's like recognizing criminals by their crimes.

INT. ALEX'S ROOM. DAY

Alex sits on his bed. Beside him are the copies of the newspaper that he brought home with the headline 'TRIPLE CORPSE HORROR'. He lifts one and tears at the front page.

*[INT. LIVING ROOM. DAY

McCall and Mitchell sit facing David. He is looking at the photographs of Hugo, Tim and Andy (as they were when alive). They are official, mug-shot snaps. David shows no hint of recognition.

DAVID

No, I've never seen them.

MCCALL

You're sure of that.

DAVID

Yes.

MCCALL

That wasn't a question.

MITCHELL

You can tell by the intonation.

MCALL

One other thing. Do you have any tattoos?

DAVID

No.

McCall points at the photograph of Tim.

*Cut from completed film.

96

MCCALL

Neither does he.

David and McCall both look at the photograph.

A small trickle of plaster and dust falls from the ceiling and lands on McCall's knee. He wipes it off and looks up. David sees but does not look up.]

INT. LIVING ROOM. DAY

McCall and Mitchell sit opposite Alex.

*[ALEX

Is this being recorded?

MCCALL

This is just an informal discussion.

ALEX

Are you recording it?

MCCALL

What does it look like?

ALEX

It looks like he's writing everything down.

MCCALL

That's because he is. Does that upset you?

ALEX

No. Why should it?

MCCALL

Well, then?]

ALEX

I've never seen any of these men before.

MCCALL

Take another look at these two.

*Cut from completed film.

ALEX

I don't know them.

MCCALL

And if I told you their car was parked outside, would that surprise you?

ALEX

Yes, I suppose so.

McCall gathers up the photographs and puts them into an inside pocket.

Well, is it?

MCCALL

What?

ALEX

Parked outside?

INT. LOFT/LIVING ROOM (FROM ABOVE). DAY

MCCALL

No, not any more. I just wondered if it would surprise you.

INT. LOFT. DAY

David steps back from the hole above the living room. He is puzzled.

INT. LIVING ROOM. DAY

Alex's interrogation continues.

MCCALL

That's it, then.

ALEX

That's all?

MCCALL

Yes. Sorry to waste your time.

ALEX

Oh, no problem. Don't worry.

MCCALL

Just one thing.

ALEX

Yes.

MITCHELL

That watch.

ALEX

What?

MCCALL

Your watch.

MITCHELL

Is it real?

MCCALL

Or a fake?

ALEX

What? Uh, no, no, it's a fake. I picked it up in Thailand. The second hand doesn't sweep, you see.

MCCALL

I see.

Mitchell takes a note of this.

ALEX

Right.

MCCALL

Tell you what. If you do remember seeing any of these guys, maybe you could give me a phone, on this number, any time you like.

He holds out a card for Alex. Alex hesitates and then takes the card.

INT. HALL. NIGHT

The hall is empty but we can hear voices from the living room.

ALEX

I didn't tell them anything. Nothing at all, absolutely nothing.

They're plods, that's all they are. If they had anything, anything at all to connect us, any witnesses, any forensic evidence, they'd have whipped it out there and then.

INT. LIVING ROOM. NIGHT

Alex, Juliet and David are in the room.

DAVID

But they know.

ALEX

They can know all they like, it won't do them the slightest bit of good –

DAVID

They know.

ALEX

They know? So what? They have nothing, there is nothing, to connect us to that bodies stuff.

DAVID

Except the money.

JULIET

He's right, Alex. They know.

INT. HALL. NIGHT

The empty hall and closed door as before.

INT. LOFT. NIGHT

The loft is dark but a small amount of light filters in, revealing David's face on the pillow. He is awake. In his hand he holds the Polaroid of Alex. He examines it, then, reaching up, he pins it to a rafter so that Alex's face stares down at him.

There is movement in the bed beside him. It is Juliet, asleep.

INT. ALEX'S ROOM. NIGHT

Alex is also awake. He sits up and reaches out for some clothes.

INT. LOFT. NIGHT

Juliet sleeps, while David slowly extricates himself from the bed.

He lifts the lid of the tank and pulls at a piece of string, on the end of which is the thick yellow plastic bag.

INT. ALEX'S ROOM. NIGHT

Faintly lit by a dimmed lamp, Alex opens the door to the hall.

INT. LOFT. NIGHT

David makes his way to the trapdoor and slowly opens it. The door creaks once and Juliet mutters in her sleep but does not wake.

INT. ALEX'S ROOM. NIGHT

Hearing the creak, Alex freezes in mid-dial, but hears nothing more. He starts to dial again, then stops and replaces the receiver but continues to hold it.

INT. HALL. NIGHT

David drops to the floor with the money.

INT. DAVID'S ROOM. NIGHT

The light is on. David dresses quickly but quietly and pulls a bag from under his bed, into which he puts some clothes, his passport, etc.

INT. ALEX'S ROOM. NIGHT

Alex lifts the receiver again and dials. He stares at a card in his hand. It is the one given to him by McCall.

INT. DAVID'S ROOM. NIGHT

David is now wearing a coat and is finished packing. He glances quickly around his room for the last time, then lifts the two bags and switches off his light.

INT. HALL. NIGHT

As David closes his door behind him he disappears into the darkness of the hall.

Suddenly he is brightly illuminated as the main light goes on.

Juliet stands by the door of the flat, dressed to leave.

JULIET

You forgot to wake me.

INT. ALEX'S ROOM. NIGHT

Alex sits still, listening to David and Juliet. He ignores the message that can be heard coming over the telephone.

WOMAN'S VOICE

This office is closed at present. In the event of an emergency, please contact the duty officer via the switchboard. If you wish to leave a message, please speak clearly after the tone, leaving your name, address and telephone number.

Over this, David and Juliet can be heard from the hall.

JULIET

So let's go.

DAVID

You and me?

INT. HALL. NIGHT

David and Juliet stand as before.

JULIET

Together.

David nods, then steps across the hall, leans down and pulls the telephone cable from its socket in the wall. He calls out to Alex.

DAVID

Hey, Alex, who are you calling at this time of night? Come on out and talk to us.

Alex appears at the door of his room. He is not angry, but wary.
Juliet is not sure what David is playing at.

Well?

Alex says nothing.

Sex lines? Is that it? Triple X-rated interactive fantasy? Old habits die hard.

ALEX
Yeah, I was phoning your mother.

DAVID
You old devil. Well, anyway, as you can see, we're leaving.

ALEX
So I gathered.

DAVID
Yeah, I'm sorry, but that's the way it is.

ALEX
It's all right. I'll forward your mail.

DAVID
No, really, I am sorry, sorry to be ducking out on you like this. I hope you won't take it personally.

ALEX
Oh, no, no, no. Don't let it worry you. Not at all. It's probably for the best.

DAVID
For the best. Exactly. I wouldn't want things to end on a downer.

ALEX
Not at all.

DAVID
I mean, we've had ups and downs, right – good times, bad times?

ALEX
Yeah.

DAVID

But more laughter than tears, I think? Yes. On balance? I mean, remember that time when – oh, we could talk all night, but we have to go. Don't we, Juliet?

JULIET

Yes.

DAVID

And you need your sleep.

ALEX

Yes.

David pauses in thought.

DAVID

No, can't think of anything else that matters.

ALEX

About the mail –

DAVID

It's very kind of you to offer, but –

ALEX

Where do you think you'll go?

DAVID

Where will we go? Where will we go? Juliet?

He turns to her.

JULIET

Eh, I don't know.

DAVID

Oh, don't be so coy, dear. You're going to Rio.

JULIET

What?

DAVID

That's right. You're going to Rio. Rio de Janeiro. On your own. Come on, you should know. You bought the fucking ticket.

David produces Juliet's airline ticket from a pocket and hands it to Alex, who looks at it before putting it in a pocket.

Do you see that? Did you know about it? I'll bet you she didn't tell you about that before she sent you up there. You could have died. What did she say, 'We'll split it together, you and me, fifty fifty'?

He turns to Juliet.

But I bet you didn't say you were going to split on him.

JULIET
It wasn't like that.

DAVID
Don't lie to me. Don't treat me like that.

ALEX
I bought it.

Juliet looks to Alex in surprise. David is momentarily confused.

DAVID
What?

ALEX
I bought the tickets. One for her and one for me. It was my idea.

DAVID
Your idea? Well, that fits. I mean, the two of you, that fits together. I should have seen that long ago.

David picks up his bags and starts walking to the door.

Juliet bars his way. He stops.

David gently shoves past her, but Juliet overtakes him and stands right in front of the door. David stops again.

JULIET
Stop him, Alex. You've got to stop him.

ALEX
Let him go. Let him take it all.

*David steps forward, but Juliet is pressed against the door. He drops
his holdall and reaches for the door handle. Juliet tries to push him
back. They struggle but neither is winning. David relaxes.*

DAVID

I'm going.

*David pauses for a moment, then hits Juliet once in the face,
knocking her to the ground.*

*David looks at her with disdain, then reaches for the door handle. As
he does so he is hit from behind by Alex. Surprised as much as hurt,
David stumbles round and touches his cheek. Alex is almost
apologetic.*

ALEX

You shouldn't have hit her. You can do whatever you like, but you
shouldn't have hit her.

*David takes a step towards the door again, but Alex launches himself
at him, forcing him back, where he trips over Juliet's outstretched leg
and drops his case. As Alex and David fight briefly on the floor,
Juliet picks up the holdall containing the money and throws it into the
kitchen.*

*David forces Alex off and, pushing past Juliet, he enters the kitchen
after the bag.*

INT. KITCHEN. NIGHT

*David stands holding the bag, but a few feet from him, Alex and
Juliet block his exit. David holds out the bag temptingly towards
Alex.*

DAVID

You want it? You want it?

*As Alex lunges at the bag, David shifts and kicks Alex in the groin,
but is himself immediately stunned again by being hit in the face with
the edge of a toaster held by Juliet.*

*A brutal and angry fight ensues, mainly between Alex and David,
around the kitchen and involving various implements and artefacts in
it.*

106

Eventually, just as Alex seems to be gaining the upper hand, David reaches out, pulls a long knife from the wooden holder and plunges it with great force through the upper part of Alex's right lung, just beneath his shoulder, pinning Alex to the wooden floor.

David sits up and reaches for a second knife but, as he does so, a blade is forced through his own throat, appearing at the front. Clutching his throat, David falls to the floor, burbling and bleeding to death.

Juliet surveys the scene with shock. She approaches Alex, who cannot reach his left arm over to the knife in his chest. They look into one another's eyes. Neither she nor Alex speaks.

As Juliet carefully touches the knife in his chest, Alex winces. With his right hand he grasps her ankle. She tries to shake herself free, but Alex holds on. She stops and takes off one of her shoes.

JULIET

You did the right thing, but I can't take you with me.

Holding the toe of her shoe, she hammers the top of the knife two or three times, driving it firmly into the floor. Alex's grip falls away. She then puts her shoe back on and picks up the bag of money.

Juliet leaves the kitchen carrying the case. Alex looks to one side,

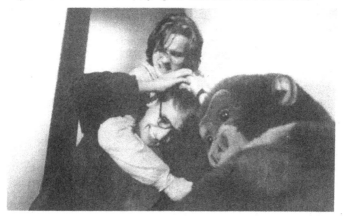

where David is breathing his last, and to the other into the hall. In the hall, he can see Juliet reappearing from her room, carrying the holdall of money and another bag. She walks back into the kitchen, kneels down and kisses Alex's forehead. At the same time, she takes the airline ticket from his pocket. She stands again and leaves. She disappears from sight and we hear the main door close.

INT. KITCHEN. NIGHT.

Alex lies alone, with David's body beside him.

INT. KITCHEN. DAY

It is brightly lit now. Policemen's legs swarm around Alex, who blinks as a flashlight fires. He looks out to the hall again, where he sees McCall and Mitchell.

Alex lies back, a faint smile on his face.

INT. KITCHEN. DAY

The handle of the knife fills the screen. Moving slowly, the picture tracks down the blade, past Alex's shoulder and down to the pine floor, then through the floorboard to the tip of the blade on the other side. A drop of blood falls from the tip, a few centimetres, on to a thick pile of banknotes.

INT. AN AIRPORT DEPARTURES HALL. DAY

Scraps of ripped newspaper lie scattered around the holdall. Two of the scraps contains the headline 'TRIPLE CORPSE HORROR'.

INT. DAY. MORGUE

A horizontal strip of face. The eyes unmoving and unblinking. We draw back to reveal David laid out on a mortuary tray.

> DAVID
> (*voice-over*)

Oh, yes, I believe in friends, I believe we need them, but if, one day, you find you just can't trust them any more, well, what then, what then?

Two attendants in white approach across the mortuary and slide the tray into its slot.

Darkness.

CREDITS

Costume Designer	Kate Carin
Sound Mixer	Colin Nicholson
Sound Editor	Nigel Galt
Casting Director	Sarah Trevis
Make-up Designer	Graham Johnston
Art Director	Zoe MacLeod
Assistant Art Director	Tracey Gallacher
Production Buyer	Karen Wakefield
Art Department Assistant	Iain Macaulay
Story Board Artist	John Amabile
First Assistant Director	Ian Madden
Second Assistant Director	Alison Goring
Third Assistant Director	Stephen Docherty
Floor Runner	Niki Longmuir
Script Supervisor	Anne Coulter
Location Manager	Fran Robertson
Production Accountant	Hilda Booth
Production Coordinator	Yvonne McParland
Production Runner	Saul Metzstein
Prop Master	Gordon Fitzgerald
Standby Props	Pat Harkins
Dressing Props	Stewart Cunningham
Props Driver	Scott Kerry
Focus Puller	Ian Jackson
Loader	Lewis Buchan
Grip	Roy Russel
Boom Operator	Tony Cook
Stills Photographers	Nigel Robertson
	Dominic Turner
Re-Recording Mixers	Brian Saunders
	Ray Merrin
Digital Sound Editor	Paul Conway
Footsteps Editor	Richard Fettes
First Assistant Editor	Anuree de Silva
Second Assistant Editor	Neil Williams
Titles Design	Morag Myerscough
Post Production Supervisor	Steve Barker
Music Supervisor	Gemma Dempsey
Special Make-up Effects	Grant Mason
Special Visual Effects	Tony Steers
Make-up Assistant	Carmel Jackson
Wardrobe Supervisor	John Norster

Stunt Arranger	Clive Curtis
Gaffer	Willie Cadden
Best Boy	Mark Ritchie
Electrician	Arthur Donnelly
Genny Operator	Derrick Ritchie
Construction Manager	Colin H. Fraser
Construction Chargehand	Derek Fraser
Standby Carpenters	Brian Adams
	Danny Sumsion
Standby Rigger	Kenny Richards
Standby Stage	Bryan Boyne
Standby Painter	Jim Patrick
Carpenters	Peter Knotts
	Richard Hassall
	John Watts
Painters	Paul Curren
	Sam Curren
Stage	Campbell Atkinson
Scenic Artist	Stuart Clark
Runners	James Stewart
	Mat Bergel
	Eric Smith
	Jamie Spencer
Trainees	Gina Lee
	Kirstin McMahon
	Dianne Jamieson

'Shallow Grave'
Written by Neil Barnes/Paul Daley
Performed by Leftfield
Courtesy of Hard Hands Ltd

'Happy Heart'
Written by James Last/Jackie Rae
Performed by Andy Williams
Published by Donna Music Ltd
Courtesy of Sony Music Entertainment Inc.

'My Baby Just Cares For Me'
Written by G. Kahn/W. Donaldson
Performed by Nina Simone
Published by EMI Music Publishing Ltd
Courtesy of Bethlehem Music

'Release The Dub'
Written by Neil Barnes/Paul Daley
Performed by Leftfield
Courtesy of Hard Hands Ltd

Television Clips

Scotland Today and *Shadowing*
Courtesy of Scottish Television PLC

Lose a Million
Courtesy of Actiontime, Carlton Television and Chris Tarrant
Carlton Music/EMI Music Publishing Ltd

The Wickerman
Courtesy of Lumière Pictures Ltd

Filmed on location in Glasgow and Edinburgh

Shallow Grave is a Film Four International and Glasgow Film Fund
presentation of a Figment Film